PRIDE, PRIDE, PRIDE

The Wisdom of the Late Brother,
President George Washington
(A True Brother)

A Book To All Readers (Free Masons and Profanes)
English | Spanish | French

CARLO CAMILLE

CONTENTS

PRIDE PRIDE PRIDE
A True Free Mason Should Not
be a Procrastinator

God, George Washington & the U.S.A. George Washington
"The Free and Accepted Mason"
of yesterday, today, and tomorrow.

*God so love the world; He chose George Washington to head s
tart themost powerful and No. 1 country in the world:
The United States of America."*

"A Book to All Readers"
"Free Masons and Profanes"

HYPOTHETICAL

In an ideal world, joining the Mason would be the best decision that a young man could make in his life. I say that not only because the great George Washington was a mason when he led our country to freedom, but also because of the great poise and growth that free masonry can offer to a young individual. Being a mason offers one the privilege to be closer to God, as well as the opportunity to get a better understanding of life, and garner life skills such as integrity, character, wisdom, clarity, entrepreneurship and a clearer conscience. Additionally, it also helps one see the world as a better place, while recognizing every human being as a creature of God. If the settler George Washington defeated the British during the Revolutionary war, it is because he was gifted by God the wisdom to formulate the future of this great country. As a mason and a member of the church, he knew that in order to achieve his task of delivering this great country from the British and granting it its independence, he had to pray at all time and lean on God's guidance throughout the entire war. In a very respectful way, George Washington is highly comparable to King Solomon, son of David in the Old Testament, whom was the wisest man of his era. They both displayed great judgement, great wisdom, as well as an immense love and respect for God which embodies everything that free masonry is about.

The life of the first president of the United States is a mystery that cannot be deciphered by any human being. Beloved late brother George Washington was born in the year of 1732 and he joined the free and accepted Mason in the year of 1752 at 20 years old. He also became a devoted member of the Presbyterian Church. During his time as a mason, he became the most respected free mason among his brothers. This type of respect combined with the guidance of God led him to become the first official commander in chief of this great country. As a free mason, George Washington firmly understood that God is the main architect of this universe. He believed that God had a plan all along to make the United States the no. 1 Country in the world through him. As a matter of fact, due to his great leadership, this belief was shared among most of his peers for almost all of the farmers or founding fathers of the United States were free and accepted mason.

Now let's talk about the lineage of free and accepted mason. Free Masonry is one of the holiest and most respected society that's ever existed. It dates all the way back to the ancient times. From the ancient times to the 18th century, God has always chosen a mason leader to lead the world in a divine fashion while simultaneously conveying his holy message to the people. For instance, God first chose Abraham to be the father of all people on earth, He then chose Moses to take His people out of Egypt and guide them to Israel, the promise land. Next, He elected to have David, a true believer of his holiness to become the King of the promise land. David then through the guidance of God passed the throne down to his son Solomon whom turned out to be the wisest King in the history of Israel. The lineage however does not stop there. It continues all the way to our beloved George Washington. God had a plan to link the United States with the new Israel otherwise known as the most prosperous nation on earth. As a result, He chose another special mason leader to be in charge. This leader was none other than George Washington. This lineage shows how sacred and special free masonry is.

A free and accepted mason in question is closer to God. As a result, when one gets closer to God, one gets a great deal of understanding and is able to decipher and solve greater challenges. One also acquires a great deal of compassion, integrity, love, respect, obedience, courage, self-control and deep faith of God's way. Free mason helps one realize the full value of life. One's life is worth nothing more than what he contributes to it. Therefore, as human being we should do our best to contribute the most we can to each other's life by continuously loving and supporting one another; for a man's life can be very hard when he is either loveless or hopeless.

George Washington embraced and embodied all the great aspects of being a free mason. It is fair to say that if George Washington was still alive, he would have been in favour of the affordable care otherwise known as Obama care. He would also be against abortion while in favour of school prayer. Furthermore, he would be neutral on gay rights, in favour of normalizing relations with Cuba, and in favour of animal rights etc. George Washington would have still been as influential as he was at that time in 18th Century. His humility was unmatched; he knew that everything in the world should be accomplished through prayer.

During the war, when King George the third found out that the person who was creating problems to his army was an ordinary settler named George Washington, he was extremely furious and surprised. He was so furious that he sent a donkey to George Washington as a way to try and humiliate him. George Washington in return accepted the donkey or (Jackass) and nicknamed the so called (Jackass) George the third. George Washington was unfazed by the King's wrongdoings and continued leading his troops to the victory that was already destined for him. The entire world took notice and witnessed the rise of George Washington.

George Washington was so loved by the American people that they wanted him to become king of the country. However, Washington was well aware that God was the one and only king in the universe and that without God's guidance, he would have never been able to lead the country to freedom. As a result, he kindly declined the American people's quest for him to become king. The bible is a synonym to free an accepted mason. God created the United States to be the center of the world where all his children would find refuge while staying away from persecution and deprivation of liberty and freedom. George Washington was God sent as the first president of the USA. As a free and accepted mason, he knew that he was being supervised and everything he did was going to be approved by God the almighty. As a result he ruled the country according to God's will.

One of his great accomplishments was the United States Capitol. When it came to the right moment to build the US capitol, which is the most sacred building to date, George Washington gathered a group of free Mason brothers with him and went to the building site and performed a ceremony of prayer to bless the building. To this day, the US Capitol still stands as tall as ever; and to many, it represents the center of the entire world.

In general all free and accepted masons should be affiliated with a church of God, which is the reason why a free mason is always closer to God. As mentioned earlier, free mason is not a religion, it is a high society and the holiest of all. Every young man twenty and older should consider joining the free masonry so that they could become a much better citizen of the great United States of America. Everybody knows that there is no spiritual life without the existence of God. From the beginning of the world God shows us how to plan for everything in life. God spiritually guided George Washington to victory against the British intruders in order to guarantee a free and greater future for the United States. God gave power to George Washington to think right and make great decisions. The relation between the United States and Israel shall never be interrupted for any reason whatsoever for God is the one who put them together. To this day, the majority of the Jews refuse to accept Jesus as the messiah. They believe in Abraham as their God. However, Abraham is not God. He was a man with a close relationship with God and as a result, God appointed him as the father of all nations. Despite their confusion, God being the loving father that he is, still blessed them with his grace as he gave them the Promised Land. God knows best. He is the past, the present and the future. Anyone who chooses to ignore his existence is making a big mistake in life for there is no life without him. God created the United States to be a Christian country; and it is and will continue to be a Christian country because this the way of God's blessing. God gave the power to the United States so they could spread peace from all over the world. The United States is the greatest power of the entire world through the grace of God. As a result, citizen of almost every third world country wants to come here for a better life.

Now let's talk about "Pope Francis." God gave us the greatest pope to represent him on earth. Pope Francis is really a man that really loves God; he is a pope who is doing his best to unite every human being on this planet. Everybody loves Pope Francis. Pope Francis says things according to the will of God. This is exactly the way George Washington used to act when he was in power. They both have allowed the love of God to guide them to do the right thing. The manner in which Pope Francis is spreading God's message these days, I'm convinced that many lost souls and atheists will soon be converted into Christianity.

During the 18th century, the era of George Washington, the free and accepted masons used to pray a lot in other for God to open the way for them so they could have perfect concentration toward the war for independence. They did so because they knew that defeating the British Army without the intervention of the almighty God was impossible. However, the impossible soon became possible as God guided George Washington and his troops toward total victory over the enemy. The British Army was left traumatized and heavily defeated for they never expected a group of settlers to even come close to defeating them. They believed that with the powerful king George on their side coupled with an arsenal of deadly ammunitions and weapons, they would easily annihilate their weak opponent. However, they failed to realize that George Washington and his troops had God on their side and that God is the one and only king of the universe. As long as one has him on their side, then nothing shall ever be deemed impossible.

God knows best at all time. God had planned to make the world a peaceful place by making the United States of America the center point to safeguard and mediate peace for all other nations. God made it that way so that everybody from every corner of the world would recognize the great United States of America as the representative of God on earth. If every one of the politicians in charge of this country today shared the same faith and belief as George Washington, they would cooperate so much better and the nation as a whole would have benefited immensely from this fruitful cooperation. When God put George Washington in charge of this country, He knew first hand that this would be his best choice for George Washington was a special vessel and through him he would be able to guide this country to the right path. As a result, one can't help but state that the United States would not have been the greatest country of them all if it wasn't for George Washington's kindness.

All the forefathers before us received their blessings from the almighty God. A good free and accepted mason knows that everyone was born to pass through eternal orient. George Washington knew that no one was perfect which is why he devoted most of his time to praying to the almighty God for more and more wisdom in order to formulate the future of America the "beautiful". Furthermore, God guided the forefathers to the site where the US capitol is standing where they prayed in order to make it a sacred building. Today, this building stands as the most sacred building in the nation. According to God, the United States of America will remain side by side with the state of Israel until the return of his son Jesus to earth. Regardless of what anyone may say, the United States is and will remain a true Christian nation for God created it as such; and what God creates, no man can ever change or destroy it.

Now let's understand the refugee situation. If George Washington was still alive, he would have been very compassionate about all refugees in general. Wherever the refugees go, they should follow the rules of that particular country and respect the people of the country as well. The refugees are human beings like any others. In every country in this world, there exists a great deal of good people and bad people. However, I believe that in general there are more good people in the world than there are bad ones. Any country that accepts to welcome refugees regardless of their place of origins shall receive more blessings from the almighty God. By doing so, these harboring countries will have fulfilled the lord's prophecy. The entire planet is under God's surveillance, therefore we all should submit to his commandments by helping one another. From the beginning of time, it was always God the father, the son and the Holy Spirit. What certain human being refused to understand is that God the father sent the son to the world to save all of us from the sins of our ancestors that began from the creation of Adam and Eve. God could have sent Jesus as a grown man like Adam, if he wanted to, but instead he chose to send him as new born so that he could grow and relate to us sinners in order to show us that things could be done the right way before saving us. Jesus was given birth by the "Virgin Mary", a faithful person who was a Jew. The story of it all remains a mystery and no one human being should try to decipher any indecipherable matter. The indecipherable shall be left to God for he is omnipotent. In the modern era, God loves the world so much that he sent George Washington, a faithful free and accepted mason and member of Presbyterian Church, to be the first president of the United States of America and head start of the most powerful nation on earth.

God created human being to be dramatically free from all over the world that is the reason he started with the United States of America. With the power that God gave to the USA, it is their duty to continue spreading the freedom as well as the democracy to every nation of the world; for freedom and democracy are equivalent to peace. Democracy is important because everyone deserves equal rights and should be treated equal under the law. George Washington did a great job establishing this foundation and God made sure that the forefathers who came after him continued the mission until today. As a result, under God's guidance, this great foundation will continue to be spread around the world and as long as God is willing, our great country will remain the most powerful among all nations.

I, the writer, was born in Haiti and the person who taught me the history of the United States and President George Washington was my godfather. My godfather was not a free mason, but he was a philosopher with a French background. He used to tell me that he loved the history of the United States and as a result proceeded to explain to me how the United Stated became an inde-

pendent country with the best system in the world. He said to me that everything happened because of God's will. He said to me that according to history,
George Washington prayed at most three times a day. He also informed about
how George Washington became a mason and member of the Presbyterian
Church. From his stories, I garnered that George Washington was a very faithful and courageous man.

After the passing of my Godfather, a friend of mine invited me to join the
free mason and as soon I received that invitation. I remembered the great
stories of my deceased Godfather and as a result, within a week, I went to the
lodge, talked to the administrator, filled out an application, and officially joined
the mason. I was 20 years old, the same age as George Washington when he
joined. As I previously wrote on the previous pages, George Washington was
a man of his era. He was really chosen by God the almighty to start the beginning of this great United States of America. My godfather once told me
if possible, follow the step of George Washington and become a free and
accepted mason. Fortunately I did so and soon after my initiation into the free
mason, I was completely transformed and became in love with the fraternity
and every single one of my close brothers. I was a changed man and I tried my
best to become a positive influence on everyone I came in contact with. To
me, free mason is the best and holiest group in society that one could associate
himself to. I also became very inspired by George Washington's story. George
Washington knew all along that God was on his side. Even when he knew that
he wouldn't be physically fit to handle certain tasks, he always believed that
God would be within him spiritually and would guide him step by step through
whatever difficult challenge put in front of him. God will always be there to
guide whoever may need his help through any difficult circumstances as long
as one believes in him. It is a big mistake for whoever choo0.292 inses to not
understand the great power of the Lord.

George Washington knew that God created every one of us to his image. Each one has a special role to play in life. Regardless of what that role may be, no human being should hate another. God put us on this planet to love one another. Whether we are rich or poor, we all belong to our savior. The reason some people do evil things is because they lack faith in God's existence. Most people think that money is the key to happiness. Others on the other hand, know that health is worth much more than money. As free masons, we believe in the latter; which is why we encourage every young man aged 20 and older to join the masonry. It will help them understand God much better. It will also help them live a much more prosperous, peaceful and meaningful life. Whoever believes in the Lord, will never be hopeless. All you have to do is continuously praise him, and call on him to make things better for you in life; and as a result, just as he did for the great George Washington, he shall do for you as well.

ORGULLO ORGULLO ORGULLO
Un Mason verdadero no debe ser indeciso

**Dios, George Washington y los Estados Unidos
George Washington "El Libre y Aceptado Mason"
de Ayer, hoy, y mañana**

Dios, de tal manera amó al mundo, Él eligió a George Washington para liderar el país más poderoso y No. 1 del mundo: Los Estados Unidos de América."

*"Un Libro para todos los lectores"
"Masones Libres y Profanos"*

Unirse al Masón, es la mejor movida que un joven hombre puede hacer en su vida, como resultado se puede acercar a Dios, tener un mejor entendimiento de la Vida, Integridad, Carácter, Sabiduría, Claridad y Conciencia Clara al ver a todo ser humano como creatura de Dios. Ser un mejor emprendedor si el colonizador George Washington pudo haber vencido a los ingleses durante la guerra revolucionaria, es porque fue dotado por Dios para formular el futuro de este Gran País. Como Masón y miembro de la iglesia, él sabía que para alcanzar su labor él tenía que rezar todo el tiempo durante la guerra revolucionaria para la Independencia del País. Ahora comparemos al Rey Solomon, hijo de David en el Viejo Testamento; él era el hombre más sabio en esa época. Así que también podría decirse, hermano, el Presidente George Washington era el Rey Solomon en ese tiempo o momento. Buen Juicio amor de Dios, el Rey Solomon era un gran pensador como George Washington, de lo contrario, podría decirse que los dos grandes hombres tenían algo en común que era el Libre y Aceptado Mason.

La vida del primer presidente de los Estados Unidos es un misterio que no puede ser descifrado por cualquier ser humano. El difunto hermano George Washington nació en el año 1732. Y se unió al libre y aceptado Mason en el año 1752 a los 20 años de edad, se convirtió en el masón más respetado entre sus hermanos, y como resultado, fue guiado por Dios a través de la oración,

se convirtió en el primer comandante en jefe de este gran país. De hecho, él sabía que un masón libre es un hombre que entiende que Dios es el principal arquitecto de este universo. Casi todos los autores o padres fundadores de los Estados Unidos eran masones libres y aceptados.

George Washington también era un miembro devoto de la Iglesia Presbiteriana, como resultado adquirió más energía para rezar, formular el futuro de América. El creía que Dios tenía un plan original para hacer a los Estados Unidos el país no. 1 en el mundo a través de él.

Ahora hablemos acerca de la conexión del libre y aceptado masón que es la sociedad más sagrada de todos los tiempos. Dios tenía planeado para 1) Abraham ser el padre de todas las personas en la tierra. 2) Moisés llevar al pueblo de Dios fuera de Egipto a la tierra prometida que es Israel. 3) David el verdadero creyente de Dios a convertirse en el amado Rey de Israel y en su último día, pasó el trono a 4) su hijo Solomon a su vez se convirtió en el Rey más sabio de la historia de Israel y amado por todo el mundo y la conexión continua hasta el siglo 18 a 5) George Washington, que fue un colonizador, ya que Dios tenía un plan para Israel que fue el lugar de nacimiento de Dios, el nombro a George Washington para estar a cargo del nuevo mundo que se convirtió en las más nuevas y prosperas naciones en la Tierra, es decir Dios nunca se equivoca y como todos los Cristianos deberían de saber que de hecho la mayoría de los hombres jóvenes deberían unirse al masón para poder convertirse en mejores ciudadanos de los Estados Unidos.

Un libre y aceptado masón en cuestión es más cercano a Dios, como entendimiento de descifrar cosas, compasión, integridad, amor para el prójimo, respetar y obedecer la ley, auto control en la vida y mejor entendimiento del camino de Dios. Y también olvidar que la vida de todos con lo que el contribuyó a eso. Continuamente deberíamos amarnos unos a otros. La vida de un hombre es muy dura cuando no tiene ayuda. Ahora hablemos del Rey Herodes. Él sabía que él era el rey más poderoso del mundo y como resultado, intento eliminar al Hijo de Dios que vino a salvar la raza humana de los pecados que había en la tierra; ya que Dios sabía antes que tenía el Rey Herodes en mente, él lo envió a otro País junto con María y José. Ninguna otra nación pudo conquistar el estado de Israel, porque dios nació allí incluso si los Israelita no reconocían a Jesús como su salvador, entonces en lugar de reconocer a Abraham; y para Jesús no hay diferencia y siempre el amor por sus hermanos y hermanas, porque esta es la tierra que les prometió.

Si George Washington estuviera vivo, se hubiera ido por el cuidado barato o el cuidado Obama, y en contra del aborto, en favor de la oración en las escuelas, el sería neutral en los derechos de los gay, en favor de normalizar las relaciones con Cuba, nunca hubiera estado de acuerdo de cerrar el gobierno por siempre un segundo. George Washington podría seguir siendo presidente de la gente como era en aquel tiempo en el siglo 18m en favor de los derechos de los animales, o la sociedad humana y la razón de todo esto, él sabía que todo en el mundo debía cumplirse por oraciones. Cuando el Rey George el tercero de Inglaterra encontró que una persona que estaba creando problemas en su ejército, fue George Washington un ordinario, se enfureció, y se sorprendió, así que envió a un burro a George Washington para aceptar el burro o su apodo que lo llamaban el (idiota) George el tercero. Mientras que el mundo entero sabía que el subirse de George Washington estaba escrito y que suficiente de Dios había puesto para ser el no. 1 en el Gran Cristo descubrió la tierra.

George Washington sabía que solo había un rey en el universo y esa era la razón por la que Dios guiaba, no aceptó ser el rey soberano incluso cuando la mayoría de la gente americana quería que lo fuera. La biblia es sinónimo de eso. Por cierto, como lo indicó la historia, cuando la mayoría de las personas del proclamado unión de George Washington para ser el rey, el gran señor se negó dejar pasar eso recordando el acto moral pasado de un rey y Salomón que era la razón por la que Dios puso palabras en la boca de George Washington para aceptar el proposición de ser rey de los Estados Unidos. Dios creó los Estados Unidos para ser el centro del mundo. Donde todos sus hijos pudieran encontrar refugio pero permaneciendo lejos de la persecución y de la depravación de la libertad. El Presidente George Washington fue enviado por Dios como el primer presidente de EEUU. El reinó el país de acuerdo al deseo de Dios. Como libre y aceptado masón, él sabía que estaba siendo supervisado para ser aprovechado por Dios el todo poderoso.

Cuando llegó el momento de construir la capital de EEUU, que es el edificio más sagrado hasta hoy de esa nación sagrada. George Washington había juntado algunos masones libres con él para ir al edificio y llevar a cabo la ceremonia de oración para que la capital representara al mundo entero. En general todos los masones libres y aceptados deben ser afiliados con la iglesia de Dios, esa es la razón por la que un masón libre está más cerca a Dios. Como ya se mencionó la libre masón no es una religión, tiene una alta sociedad y la más sagrada de todas. Cada hombre de 20 años de edad o más. Debe unirse a la libre masonería para que sean mejores ciudadanos para los Grandes Estados Unidos de América. Ya como todos saben que no hay vida espiritual sin la existencia de Dios. Desde el principio del mundo Dios mostró como planear todo en la vida con la santa trinidad; Dios en tres personas separadas que son de nuevo iguales a uno que llamamos misterio de la santa trinidad. De nuevo Dios detectó George Washington con la victoria contra el intruso Británico para formular el futuro de los Estados Unidos. Dios le dio el poder a George Washington para pensar bien y hacer una buena decisión. La relación entre los Estados Unidos e Israel nunca debe cesar o ser interrumpida por cualquier razón porque Dios es quien los unió incluso, la mayoría de los judíos no quiere aceptar que Jesús es el mesías, pero aún están bendecidos por la gracia de Dios como les dio la tierra prometida. Los judíos creían en Abraham, y él no es Dios, él era un hombre, que tenía una relación cercana con Dios y él lo nombre el padre de todas las naciones. Como George Washington era el padre de todos los ciudadanos de Estados Unidos. Dios sabe mejor, pasado presente y futuro. Cualquiera que ignore la existencia de Dios comete un gran error en la vida porque no hay vida sin Él.

Dios ha creado a los Estados Unidos para ser un país Cristiano, y es un país Cristiano y continuara siendo un país Cristiano, porque este es el camino a la bendición de Dios. Dios le dio poder a los Estados Unidos para que pudieran hablar de paz en todo el mundo. Los Estados Unidos son el poder más grande de todo el mundo a través de la gracia de Dios. Por consiguiente, casi todos los ciudadanos de un país tercermundista quisieran venir aquí para tener una mejor vida. Ahora hablemos acerca del "Papa Francisco". Dios nos dio al mejor papa para representarlo a él en la tierra el Papa Francisco es un hombre que realmente ama a Dios, él es un papa que hace lo mejor para unir a todos los seres humanos en este planeta. Todo el mundo ama al Papa Francisco. El Papa Francisco dice las cosas de acuerdo a la voluntad de Dios. Esta es la forma exacta en la que George Washington solía actuar cuando estaba en el poder, por el amor de Dios, hace lo correcto del dictado y la guía de Dios. La manera en la que el Papa Francisco está actuando estos días, muchos ateos se convertirán al catolicismo.

Dios ha creado 5 continentes en el mundo pero Estados Unidos reconoce 6 continentes al dividir el Continente Americano incluyendo a Norte y Sur América. En el siglo VIII la oreja de George Washington, los masones libres y aceptados solían rezar mucho para que Dios abriera un camino para ellos, para que pudieran tener una concentración perfecta referente a la guerra de la independencia. Por cierto, los guerreros sabían que no sería posible derrotar al Ejército Británico sin Dios Todopoderoso. Como ya mencionamos, Dios creo a George Washington para ser la cabeza de la nación y lo guio hacia la victoria total sobre el enemigo. El enemigo mismo no sabía si los colonizadores podían derrotarlo. El ejercito de Washington tenia a Dios de su lado y el Ejército Británico creía en su arsenal de espiritualidad. Así que ellos fallaron en comprender que Dios es el rey de todos los reyes terrenales. El Rey George el tercero en ese momento de la Revolución Americana no se esperaba la derrota por los colonizadores americanos.

Dios sabe lo mejor en todo momento, y es capaz de leer la mente de todo el mundo porque él es el único Dios que creo a los humanos y todo lo demás. Así que Dios planeo hacer al mundo un lugar pacifico al hacer que los Estados Unidos de América fueran el punto central para salvaguardar y mediar para todas las otras naciones. Dios lo hizo para que, todos los humanos de cada esquina del mundo reconocieran que los EEUU son la representación de Dios en la tierra. Si todos los gobernantes de este país tuvieran la misma fe como la de George Washington, la cooperación entre ellos, pudo haber beneficiado a los habitantes de este país. Cuando Dios puso a George Washington como encargado de este país, Él sabía de primera mano que era la mejor decisión que pudo tomar. Como todos saben en ese momento George Washington, se unió a los masones a los veinte años de edad y a través de las oraciones Dios lo guio en el camino correcto y también miembro de la Iglesia Presbiteriana. El hecho es que los Estados Unidos no habrían sido los mejores de todos si no hubiese sido como fue.

Comprender a los antepasados antes de nosotros y ellos recibieron sus bendiciones de Dios Todopoderoso. Un masón bueno libre y aceptado sabe que todos nacieron para discutir por el eterno oriente. George Washington sabía que nadie es perfecto es por eso que dedico la mayoría de su tiempo a rezar a Dios Todopoderoso para más y más sabiduría para formar el futuro de esta gran tierra América "la hermosa". Además, Dios guio a los antepasados al lugar en donde la capital de los EEUU se suponía que estuviera y ellos rezaron a Dios en el sitio de la capital que lo hizo un edificio sagrado, es decir el mas más sagrado edificio en la nación. Según Dios, los Estados Unidos de América permanecerán lado a lado con el estado de Israel hasta que regrese Jesús a la tierra. Los Estados Unidos son una verdadera nación cristiana, sin importar lo que la gente diga. Porque Dios lo creo para eso. Loque Dios le da a alguien como regalo nadie lo puede falsificar.

Ahora entendamos la situación de los refugiados. Si George Washington estuviera vivo, habría sido muy compasivo sobre todos los refugiados en general, pero a donde vayan los refugiados; ellos deben seguir las reglas de ese país en particular, respeto por las personas del país donde se establecen. Los refugiados son humanos como cualquier otro. El país de todo el mundo tiene gente buena y mala en general hay más personas buenas en el mundo entero que malas. Por cierto, cualquier país que acepte darles la bienvenida a los refugiados, sin importar el lugar de origen, debe recibir más bendiciones del Dios todopoderoso. Hacer eso, los países habrán cumplido la profecía de Dios, el planeta entero es el único donde los humanos están bajo Dios, así que todos deberíamos regirnos sobre sus mandamientos, ayudándonos el uno al otro. Cuando Dios creó al primer ser humano que fue Adán, él lo creó a su imagen y semejanza de la tierra y no fue creado como un pequeño bebé como "Presidente George Washington" el hombre con la fe masónica, Yo, su escritor, un masón libre de fe y todos los hermanos, con fe masónica libre.

Por cierto, la fe masónica mundial, significa "cercano a Dios, el creador". Jesús ha existido siempre con su padre y el espíritu santo desde el principio de los tiempos. Lo que cierto ser humano se negó a entender que el padre tuvo que enviar al hijo al mundo para salvarnos de los pecados de nuestro antecesor que comenzó desde la creación de Adán y Eva. Dios pudo haber

enviado a Jesús como un hombre crecido como Adán, si hubiera querido, pero "repetir" en otro para salvarnos, Jesús tendría que nacer de un ser humano para que el mundo fuera salvado. El humano era la "virgen maría", una persona fehaciente que era judía. Ningún ser humano debería intentar disipar cualquier cosa por nada del mundo. Deja todo a Dios porque él es omnipotente. Dios ama al mundo tanto que envío a George Washington. Dios ama al mundo, él envió a George Washington, el primer presidente de los Estados

Unidos de América, fehaciente libre y aceptó a masón como miembro de la iglesia Presbiterana; para ser el jefe de la nación más poderosa de la tierra.

Dios creó al ser humano para que fuera dramáticamente libre en todo el mundo, esa es la razón por la que comenzó con los Estados Unidos de América. Con el poder que Dios le dio a EEUU ellos podrían continuar repartiendo las palabras de libertad, y democracia para cualquier nación del mundo que no tiene la razón de la libertad y democracia igual a la paz, seguido de las reglas de la ley. Todos saben que, las reglas de la ley son esenciales, así que nadie puede vivir y hacer su deber cívico sin ellas.

Para entender la importancia del masón libre y aceptado, "cada hombre con 20 años o más debe unirse al masón que es la sociedad más sagrada entre ellos; y cuando ellos aprendan más sobre eso como George Washington. Como ejemplo, George Washington, se unió al masón a la edad de 20años en el año 1752, y nación en 1732, se hizo presidente en 1789 e inauguró en Nueva York y se muró en casa en 1799. Entre 1752 y 1799 hizo todo bien ante los ojos de Dios. Los padres que vinieron a buscarlo continuaron su misión hasta hoy. Así que mientras Dios esté dispuesto a nuestro gran país permanecerá el más poderoso en todas las naciones.

Yo, el escritor, nací en Haití, y la persona que me enseño la historia de los Estados Unidos y el Presidente George Washington; fue mi padrino y maestro y en pleno Haití que es el idioma Haitiano principal. Mi padrino no fue un masón libre, pero era un filósofo con un fondo francés, me contaba que amaba la historia de Estados Unidos y me explicaba como los Estados Unidos se volvieron independientes con el resto del sistema en el mundo, él dijo que todo pasó de Dios por George Washington y su equipo. Él me dijo que de acuerdo a la historia George Washington rezaba al menos 3 veces por día como mesón y miembro de la iglesia Presbiteriana y fue fiel y muy fuerte. Después de que murió mi abuelo, un amigo me dijo, Carlo, porque no te unes al masón libre, y de pronto vino a mí a la enseñanza de mi padrino muerto, justo dentro de una semana, había ido a ayudar con el administrador y llené una aplicación, me uní al mesón dentro de un mes a la edad de 20 años la misma que cuando George Washington se unió. Con previamente lo escribí en las páginas anteriores que George Washington era un hombre de la era fue realmente elegido por Dios todo poderoso para comenzar el principio de su gran Estados Unidos de América junto con sus colaboraciones. Recuerdo que mi padrino me dijo que si era posible, siguiera el paso de George Washington convirtiéndome en un rostro y aceptara a masón como el masón libre como el mejor y el más sagrado de la sociedad que uno podría infiltrarse. La Sociedad de: integridad, disciplina, coraje, esperanza, personalidad, inteligencia y amor los unos por los otros para el amor de Dios. Sin más, cerca del el día después de mi iniciación en el masón libre, estaba completamente transformado y me convertí en amor de fraternidad hacia todos a mi alrededor, comenzando con mi familia inmediata, amigos y cualquier ser humano con quien me contacté. Sin más, inspiré la vida del Presidente George Washington, como un gran ser humano con la bendición de Dios todo poderoso. George Washington sabía que Dios estaba de su lado y también sabía que no lo iba a ayudar físicamente con su tarea, pero espiritualmente estaba con el paso a paso hacia el difícil viaje frente a él. Por cierto Dios no ayudaba a nadie físicamente por el otro lado, enviaba sus ángeles para guiar a quien quisiera cumplir cualquier tarea que quiere que se cumpla. Así todos sabían que George Washington era la persona elegida para hacerlo a través de Dios. Es un gran error para alguien no entender el gran poder del Señor.

George Washington sabía que Dios creó a cada uno de nosotros a su imagen y cada uno tiene un rol especial en la vida, sin importar que tal papel y eso es decir que ningún ser humano debería odiar otro dios nos puedo en este planeta para amarnos, rico a pobre, porque todos pertenecemos a nuestro salvador.

La razón por la que la gente hace cosas malas, es porque no tienen existencia de Dios. Y por cierto la mayoría de las personas piensan que el dinero es el último resultado, mientras que cierta porción de las personas piensan lo contrario ya que saben que la salid de alguien vale más que el oro que es la razón por que liberamos los masones descubiertos que cada joven de edad de 20 años o más debe unirse a los masones para entender a Dios mejor de lo que lo hacen al momento y vivir una vida prospera en paz consigo mismos, especialmente cuando no tienen salida. Pero quien sea que crea en el Señor, nunca estará desamparado todo lo que tienes que hacer es alabarlo, llamarlo para hacer las cosas bien en la vida.

FIERTE FIERTE FIERTE
Un vrai maçon ne doit pas être un procrastinateur

Dieu, George Washington et les Etas Unis
George Washington
"Un franc maçon d'hier, d'aujourd'hui et de demain

Dieu a tellement aimé le monde; il a choisi George Washington pour faire démarrer le pays numéro 1 au monde: les Etats-Unis d'Amérique.

"«Un Livre pour tous les Lecteurs»
«Les Franc Maçons et les Profanes»

HYPOHTETIQUE

Rejoindre les maçons est la meilleure des choses qu'un jeune homme ait pu faire dans sa vie. Ainsi, vous devenez plus proche de Dieu, vous avez une meilleure compréhension de la vie, de l'intégrité, du caractère, de la sagesse et de la conscience claire en voyant chaque être humain en tant que créature de Dieu. Etre un meilleur entrepreneur si le colon George Washington aurait pu battre les Britanniques durant la guerre de révolution, c'est parce qu'il avait un don de Dieu afin de former le future de son pays. En tant que franc maçon et membre de l'église, il savait qu'afin de réaliser son rêve, il devait prier tout le temps durant la guerre de révolution pour obtenir l'indépendance de son pays. À présent, comparons le roi Salomon, fils de David dans l'ancien testament; il fut l'homme le plus sage de son ère. En termes de comparaison, nous pouvons dire que le Président George Washington était le Roi Salomon en ce temps-là. Le bon jugement de l'amour de Dieu, le Roi Salomon était un grand penseur tout comme George Washington. Ainsi, ils avaient quelque chose en commun, en tant que deux grands hommes.

Le premier président de la vie des Etats-Unis est un mystère et il ne peut être déchiffré par un être humain. Le bien-aimé frère George Washington est né en l'an 1732. Il a rejoint les Francs-Maçons en 1752, à l'âge de 20 ans, il

est devenu le plus respecté des Francs-Maçons parmi ses frères et, étant guidé par Dieu à travers la prière, il est devenu le premier commandant en chef de ce grand pays. Ainsi, il comprit qu'un franc-maçon est un homme qui comprend que Dieu est l'architecte principal de cet univers. Presque tous les pères fondateurs des Etats-Unis furent des francs-maçons libres et agrées.

George Washington était également un membre dévoué de l'Eglise Presbytérienne, de laquelle il a obtenu plus d'énergie pour prier et pour former la future des Etats-Unis. Il croyait que Dieu avait un plan pour faire des Etats-Unis le pays nr 1 au monde à travers lui.

A présent, parlons des liens entre les maçons libres et agrées, qui font partie de la société la plus sainte de tous les temps. Dieu avait planifié pour 1) Abraham d'être 1) le père de tous les gens vivant sur terre 2) Moïse de faire sortir les gens en dehors d'Egypte vers la terre promise d'Israël 3) David le vrai croyant de Dieu de devenir le Roi d'Israël et qui a passé son trône à 4) son fils Salomon qui devint le roi le plus sage d'Israël et aimé du monde entier. Le lien s'est poursuivi jusqu'au 18ème siècle jusqu'à 5) George Washington, qui était un colon, puisque Dieu avait un plan pour Israël, qui était le lieu de naissance de Dieu, il a chargé George Washington du nouveau monde, qui est devenu la nouvelle et plus prospères des nations sur Terre. Ainsi, Dieu n'est jamais faux et tous les Chrétiens devraient rejoindre les maçons afin de devenir de meilleurs citoyens des Etats-Unis.

Un maçon libre et agrée est plus proche de Dieu, avec une meilleure compréhension, compassion, intégrité et amour pour son prochain, respect et obéissance de la loi, courageux et contrôle de soi-même dans la vie et une meilleure compréhension de la voie de Dieu. Nous devons constamment aimer l'un l'autre. La vie de l'homme est très difficile lorsqu'il n'y trouve pas d'espoir. Parlons à présent du Roi Hérode. Il savait qu'il était le roi le plus puissant au monde et de ce fait, il a tenté d'éliminer le fil de Dieu qui était venu pour sauver la race humaine des péchés. Vu que Dieu savait ce qui se trottait dans la tête d'Hérode, il l'a envoyé dans un autre pays avec Marie et Joseph. Aucune autre nation ne pouvait conquérir l'état d'Israël car Dieu était né là-bas et même si les Israélites ne le reconnaissaient pas comme leur sauveur, ils ont reconnu Abraham à la place; et pour Jésus, ceci ne faisait aucune différence car il aimait ses frères et sœurs sur la terre qui leur était promise.

Si George Washington était toujours en vie, il aurait choisi l'assurance maladie Obama, il serait contre l'avortement et pour la prière à l'école. Il serait neutre sur les droits des homosexuels, en faveur de la normalisation des relations avec le Cuba et il n'aurait jamais été d'accord de désactiver le gouvernement ne serait-ce qu'une seconde. George Washington aurait pu être le président de tout le monde comme si c'était le 18ème siècle, il serait en faveur des droits des animaux, ou de la société humaine, la raison pour ceci est qu'il savait que tout dans ce monde peut s'accomplir à travers la prière. Lorsque le Roi George III d'Angleterre comprit que la personne qui créait des problèmes à son armée était George Washington, un colon ordinaire, il devait furieux et surpris. Ainsi, il envoyât son âne à George Washington, qui lui donna le nom de George III. Le monde entier a compris que la montée de George Washington était écrite et que Dieu l'a placé en tant que numéro 1 des colons de la nouvelle terre découverte.

George Washington savait qu'il n'y avait qu'un seul Roi et c'est la raison pour laquelle à travers la guidance de Dieu, il n'a pas accepté d'être le roi que la majorité de gens des Etats-Unis voulaient qu'il soit. Le Seigneur a refusé que ceci se passe en rappelant la morale du Roi Salomon et c'est la raison pour laquelle Dieu a mis les mots dans la bouche de George Washington afin qu'il accepte la proposition de devenir Roi des Etats Unis. Dieu a créé les Etats Unis afin qu'ils deviennent le centre du monde. En tant que maçon libre, il savait qu'il était supervisé et qu'il devait prendre ce qui lui venait de Dieu.

Lorsque le bon moment pour construire la capitale des Etats-Unis était venu, George Washington avait rassemblé quelques francs-maçons avec lui afin qu'ils aillent sur le lieu de la construction et qu'ils prient pour que la capitale représente le centre du monde. En général, tous les maçons devaient faire partie d'une église de Dieu et c'est la raison pour laquelle un franc-maçon est proche de Dieu. Comme il l'a déjà été mentionné, la franc- maçonnerie n'est pas une religion, c'est une haute société et la plus sainte de tous. Chaque jeune homme de 20 ans et plus pouvait y faire partie. Lorsqu'ils rejoignaient les francs-maçons, ils devenaient de meilleurs citoyens des grands Etats-Unis d'Amérique. Comme tout le monde le sait, il n'y a pas de vie spirituelle sans l'existence de Dieu. Depuis le début du monde, Dieu nous montre comme tout planifier dans la vie grâce à la trinité. Dieu en trois personnes séparées ce que nous appelons le mystère de la trinité. Encore une fois, Dieu a prédit à George Washington la victoire contre l'intrus britannique afin de former la future des Etats-Unis. Dieu a donné du pouvoir à George Washington afin de penser comme il fallait et de prendre de bonnes décisions. La relation entre les Etats-Unis et Israël ne doit jamais cesser ni s'interrompre pour quelconque raison car Dieu est celui qui les a placés ensemble, même si la majorité des Juifs ne veulent pas accepter Jésus en tant que Messie. Ils sont toujours considérés comme bénis car Dieu leur a donné la terre promise. Les juifs croyaient en Abraham, et il n'est pas Dieu, il n'était qu'un homme qui avait une bonne re-lation avec Dieu et c'est pour cela qu'il l'a élu père de toutes les nations, tout comme George Washington était le père de chaque citoyen des Etats-Unis. Dieu connaît le mieux le présent, le passé et le futur. Quiconque ignore l'existence de Dieu fait une grande erreur dans la vie car il n'y a pas de vie sans lui.

Dieu a créé les Etats-Unis afin qu'ils deviennent un pays chrétien, et c'est un pays chrétien qui continuera de l'être, car c'est de cette façon que Dieu l'a béni. Dieu a donné le pouvoir aux Etats Unis afin qu'ils puissent étendre la paix dans le monde. Les Etats-Unis sont le plus grand pouvoir du monde grâce à Dieu. De ce fait, presque tous les citoyens des pays du tiers-monde veulent venir ici pour une vie meilleure. Parlons à présent du pape François. Dieu nous a donné le plus grand des papes afin de le représenter sur terre. Le Pape François est vraiment un homme qui aime vraiment Dieu, c'est un pape qui fait son meilleur pour unifier chaque être humain de cette planète. Tout le monde apprécie le pape François. C'est exactement la façon dont George Washington gouvernait lorsqu'il était au pouvoir, avec l'amour de Dieu, il faisait les bonnes choses selon ce que Dieu conseillait. La façon dont le pape François agit ces jours fera convertir beaucoup d'athées au catholicisme.

Dieu a créé les 5 continents dans le monde mais les Etats-Unis reconnaissent 6 continents en divisant le continent Américain, celui du Sud et du Nord. Au 8ème siècle, les maçons priaient beaucoup afin que Dieu puisse leur montrer la voie, ainsi ils pourraient avoir une concentration parfaite lors de la guerre pour l'indépendance. Dieu sait tout mieux que chacun et il est capable de lire la pensée de chacun car il est le seul et l'unique Dieu qui a créé les humains et tous ce qui les entoure. Ainsi, Dieu avait planifié de faire de la Terre un endroit pacifique en faisant des Etats-Unis le point central de la Terre. Dieu l'a fait ainsi, tous les êtres humains de chaque coin du monde reconnaissent que les Etats-Unis sont les représentants de la vie de Dieu sur Terre. Si tous les dirigeants de ce pays seraient comme George Washington, la coopération entre eux serait meilleure et les habitants auraient obtenu plus de bénéfices. Lorsque Dieu a chargé George Washington de ce pays, il a su tout d'abord que ce serait le meilleur choix qu'il ait fait. Comme chacun le sait, en ce temps-là, George Washington a rejoint les francs-maçons à l'âge de 20 ans et à travers la prière, Dieu l'a amené dans le droit chemin et a fait de lui un membre de l'église Presbytérienne.

Il faut comprendre que les ancêtres ont reçu leurs bénédictions de Dieu tout-puissant. Un bon maçon sait que toute personne n'était né pour passer à travers l'orient éternel. George Washington savait que personne n'est parfait et c'est pour cela qu'il a dévoué tout son temps à prier Dieu tout-puissant pour plus en plus de sagesse afin de former le futur de la belle Amérique. De plus, Dieu a guidé les ancêtres vers l'endroit où la capitale des Etats-Unis était supposée être et ils ont prié Dieu sur le site de la capitale et c'est ce qui en a fait un immeuble sacré. Selon Dieu, les Etats-Unis d'Amérique vont toujours rester côte à côte avec l'état d'Israël jusqu'au retour de Jésus sur Terre. Les Etats Unis sont une vraie nation, peu importe ce qui se dit. Parce que c'est Dieu qui l'a créé ainsi et personne ne peut le falsifier.

À présent, tentons de comprendre la situation des réfugiés. Si George Washington était toujours en vie, il aurait été très passionné à propos des réfugiés en général, mais peu importe où les réfugiés vont, ils doivent respecter les personnes du pays où ils vont. Ce sont des êtres humains tout comme les autres. Tous les pays du monde ont des gens bien et des gens mauvais mais en général ce sont les bonnes gens qui sont en majorité. Tout pays qui accepte d'accueillir des réfugiés reçoit plus de bénédictions de la part du tout-puissant. En faisant ceci, les pays auront ainsi atteint la prophétie. Lorsque Dieu crée Adam, il l'a créé à son image, en tant que personne s'étant développée de la boue il n'a pas été créé comme un petit bébé tel que le « Président George Washington », l'homme avec une foi maçonnique totale.

Cependant, les mots foi maçonnique totale signifient « proche de Dieu, le créateur ». Jésus a existé à travers son père et l'esprit saint depuis le début des temps. Ce que certains êtres humains ont refusé de comprendre, c'est que le père avait envoyé son fils dans le monde pour nous sauver. Dieu aurait pu envoyer Jésus comme un homme grand tel que Adam, si il le voulait mais il a « répété » parce qu'il voulait que Jésus le sauveur vienne être humain. Cet être humain était la « vierge Marie », une personne pleine de foi et qui était juive. Personne ne devrait tenter de déchiffrer quelque chose de déchiffrable? Laissons tout ceci à Dieu car il est omnipotent. Dieu a tellement aimé le monde qu'il a envoyé George Washington, le premier président des Etats-Unis, un franc-maçon libre et plein de foi et un membre de l'église Presbytérienne afin qu'il soit le démarreur de la plus grande nation sur Terre.

Dieu a créé l'être humain afin qu'il soit dramatiquement libre partout sur Terre et c'est la raison pour laquelle il a commencé avec les Etats-Unis d'Amérique. Avec le pouvoir que Dieu a donné aux USA, ils pourraient continuer à disperser la liberté et la démocratie à chaque nation du monde qui ne possède pas ces attributs. Chacun sait que les règles venant de la loi sont essentielles ainsi personne ne pourrait vivre civiquement sans elles.

Chaque jeune homme de 20 ans et plus pouvait y faire partie. Lorsqu'ils rejoignaient les francs-maçons, ils devenaient de meilleurs citoyens des grands Etats-Unis d'Amérique. Par exemple, George Washington a rejoint les maçons à l'âge de 20 ans en 1752, il était né en 1732, devenu président en 1789 et inaugura New York avant de mourir à la maison en 1799. Entre 1752 et 1799, il a réalisé le souhait du seigneur. Les descendants qui sont arrivés après lui continuent la mission aujourd'hui. Donc, tant que Dieu le voudra, notre pays restera la nation la plus puissante.

Moi, l'auteur, je suis né en Haïti et la personne qui m'a appris l'histoire des Etats-Unis et de George Washington était mon parrain en langue Créole, qui est la langue principale de Haïti. Mon parrain n'était pas un franc-maçon mais il était un philosophe aux très bonnes connaissances de français. Il me disait souvent qu'il aimait l'histoire des Etats-Unis et il m'expliquait comment les Etats-Unis sont devenus un pays indépendant avec le meilleur système au monde. Il disait que tout était arrivé de la part de Dieu à travers George Washington et son équipe. Il me disait que selon l'histoire, George Washington priait trois fois par jour en tant que maçon et membre de l'église Presbytérienne. Il était très courageux.

Après la mort de mon parrain, l'un de mes amis et venu et m'a dit « Carlo, pourquoi ne rejoins-tu pas le franc-maçon », après avoir compris que j'avais absorbé les enseignements de mon parrain décédé. Après une semaine, j'ai décidé d'aller dans la loge et de discuter avec l'administrateur. J'ai rejoint ensuite les francs-maçons à l'âge de 20 ans, au même âge que George Washington. Comme je l'ai écrit auparavant, George Washington était un homme de l'ère et il a été choisi par Dieu le tout-puissant afin d'être le démarreur des Etats-Unis. Je me souviens que mon parrain disait que si c'était possible, il fallait que je suive les pas de Georges Washington en devenant un maçon respecté et accepté. C'est la société: de l'intégrité, du courage, de l'espoir, de la personnalité, de l'intelligence et de l'amour pour chacun ainsi que pour l'amour de Dieu. De plus, j'étais complètement transformé et devient amoureux de la fraternité envers chacun autour de moi en commençant par ma famille, mes amis et chaque être humain. Plus tard, je me suis inspiré de la vie de George Washington en tant que grand être humain à travers les bénédictions de Dieu tout-puissant. George Washington savait que Dieu était avec lui et il savait qu'il allait l'aider physiquement dans ses quêtes. Dieu n'aide personne physiquement mais il lui envoie ses anges afin de le/la guider dans l'accomplissement de ses tâches. Comme nous le savons tous, George Washington était la personne choisie par Dieu pour accomplir les tâches. C'est une grande erreur que de ne pas comprendre le grand pouvoir de Dieu.

George Washington savait que Dieu nous a créé chacun à son image et chacun a un rôle spécial à jouer dans la vie, peu importe lequel. Aucun être humain ne doit haïr son prochain. Dieu nous a placés sur cette planète pour nous aimer, que l'on soit riche ou pauvres, parce que nous appartenons tous à notre Seigneur. La raison pour laquelle certaines personnes font de mauvaises choses c'est parce qu'ils ne connaissent pas l'existence de Dieu. La majorité des gens pensent que l'argent et le meilleur résultat alors qu'une autre partie pense le contraire puisqu'ils savent que la santé de chacun est plus importante que l'or et c'est la raison pour laquelle nous, les francs-maçons, avons découvert que chaque jeune homme de 20 ans et plus doit nous rejoindre afin de mieux comprendre Dieu, surtout lorsque la vie est difficile ou qu'une personne est sans espoir. Mais quiconque croit en Dieu ne sera jamais sans espoir et tout ce qu'il vous reste à faire est de le louer, se souvenir de lui afin de rendre les choses meilleures dans la vie.

PRIDE PRIDE PRIDE

PRIDE PRIDE PRIDE

Printed in the USA
CPSIA information can be obtained
at www.ICGtesting.com
CBHW071034271124
18028CB00042B/452